AI and Cyber Warfare
New Terrain and Tactics for Defense

Table of Contents

Chapter 1. Introduction

In this compelling Special Report, we delve into the complex and increasingly crucial crossroads of AI and Cyber Warfare, a new terrain that's continuously reshaping the defense tactics of the modern world. The realm of cyber warfare has already evolved beyond our traditional understanding, and with the onset of artificial intelligence, the rules of engagement are being rewritten. This might sound complex, but rest assured, we've broken it down in a straightforward, accessible manner. By dipping your toes in this report, you'll not only unravel the intricate blend of technology and strategy, but you'll also gain a substantial insight into how AI is transforming cyber defense, enriching your understanding and readying you for the future. Committing to this Special Report is embarking on a journey that provides an invaluable perspective for anyone interested in technology, security, or the future of global defense.

Chapter 2. Artificial Intelligence: A brief introduction

Artificial intelligence (AI) denotes the simulation of human intelligence within machines that are designed and programmed to think like humans, and imitate their actions. The term may also apply to a machine that exhibits characteristics emulating human mind such as learning and problem-solving.

2.1. Understanding AI - Basic Concepts

Artificial intelligence lays its roots from the field of computer science, focusing on creating an automated system of 'intelligent agents', able to perceive their environment and take actions leading to its success. This enables AI to achieve goals, ranging from understanding complex languages to recognizing emotions, and much more.

AI is typically classified into two main types, 'Narrow AI', designed and trained to carry out a specific task such as voice commands, and 'General AI', that can understand, learn and apply knowledge across a multitude of tasks.

2.2. AI and Its Historical Timeline

The birth of AI dates backs to 1956, when it was first coined by John McCarthy, a computer scientist, in the historic Dartmouth conference. During the 1960s and 1970s, the light of AI started fading with the lack of progress, until in 1980s, when British Governments started funding AI again with an aim to compete against the Japanese fifth-generation computer project.

After a brief quiet period in the 1990s, AI sparked back into life in the 21st century, boosted by the rise in computing power and data, alongside the birth of machine learning and AI subsets such as neural networks and natural language processing.

2.3. Excavating the Foundations: Algorithms and Machine Learning

Underneath the AI umbrella lies Machine Learning (ML), where computer systems are given the ability to learn and improve from experience without being explicitly programmed. Machine Learning algorithms, often referred to as 'models', use computational methods to "learn" information from data. They can then make predictions or decisions without being specifically directed to do so.

These algorithms are typically categorized into three types, 'Supervised Learning', where the model learns from labeled data; 'Unsupervised Learning', where the model figures out patterns from input data without any labels; and 'Reinforcement Learning', involving a model that learns via interacting with its environment.

2.3.1. Deep Learning: A Leap Further

A subset of Machine Learning is Deep Learning. It uses a layered structure of algorithms called neural networks, inspired by the human brain. With an immense capacity for learning, deep learning algorithms execute data processing tasks such as pattern recognition and feature extraction, teaching themselves to carry out intricate processes by exposure to large datasets.

It was the development and refinement of deep learning models that drove the rapid evolution of AI over the last decade. Deep learning allowed AI systems to handle larger data sets in a much more efficient manner, handling complex tasks seamlessly that were previously insurmountable.

2.4. AI Applications: From Everyday Use to Advanced Computation

We now live in a world where AI technology is not just a novel concept, but an integral part of our daily lives. From recommendation engines fueling our entertainment on Netflix, to helping diagnose diseases and eradicating spam emails, AI is revolutionizing multiple business sectors.

Simultaneously, AI is empowering advanced sectors such as autonomous vehicles, which not only operate using sensors and ongoing machine learning but can also predict, judge, and make decisions—key aspects of human cognition.

2.5. Future Perspectives and the Upcoming Challenges

As AI continues its rapid progression, the future abounds with possibilities. Experts foresee AI further embedding into our lives, potentially contributing to humanitarian causes like climate change and healthcare but it's also inevitably going to cause significant disruption.

The ethical implications of AI are causing serious debates, centered around data privacy, socio-economic inequality, and autonomy. AI also casts a mammoth question over the future of work and employment, as jobs become increasingly automated.

In summary, AI has come a long way since its inception - a journey fraught with ups and downs. Its future seems equally turbulent and promising, as we grapple with its extraordinary capabilities and potential consequences. This rich and colourful tapestry of AI forms the foundation and preface to its pivotal role in the realm of Cyber Warfare, as we will explore in the subsequent chapters of this report.

Chapter 3. The Evolution of Cyber Warfare

In the early years of the internet, the concept of warfare stretched only as far as physical combat, using tangible tools and weapons. However, in recent decades, this landscape has dramatically expanded to fight battles that exist in the intangible realm of cyberspace. This transformation is due to rapid technological advancements which have brought us to the brink of a new era - the age of cyber warfare, where battles are fought behind keyboards and screens. This chapter will traverse the course of this evolution, highlighting milestones, as well as the strengths and vulnerabilities of our new digital battlefields.

3.1. The Dawn of the Digital Battlefield

The internet started as an innocuous web of interconnected computers. Conceived in the 1960s, its original purpose was to facilitate communication by linking various computer networks. As the nascent World Wide Web, or "Cyberspace," became more complex and accessible, so did its vulnerabilities. In the 1980s, the first instances of exploiting these vulnerabilities emerged as computer viruses, designed to disrupt or damage computer systems. These were rudimentary engagements in cyber warfare, and they planted the seeds for the escalating clashes that we face today.

3.2. The Rise of Cyber Attacks

As the internet evolved, so did the techniques used to exploit it. Cyber Command of the United States Department of Defense coined the term "Cyber Warfare" to reflect a new breed of attacks that targeted state infrastructures, leveraging digital tools for strategic military purposes. One prominent early example of cyber warfare was the "Moonlight Maze" operation by an unknown foreign entity in the mid-1990s. It targeted United States military and government networks, exfiltrating valuable and sensitive data.

Simultaneously, non-state actors, like hackers and cybercriminals, also began using the internet for personal gain or ideological purposes. Their tactics evolved from rudimentary Distributed Denial-of-Service (DDoS) attacks to more sophisticated ransomware and data breaches. Every device connected to the internet became a potential target, vulnerability, or tool for cyber warfare.

3.3. Cyber Espionage and State Actors

In the 2000s, the role of state actors came to the forefront of cyber warfare. Cyber espionage emerged as a strategic tool for nations to gain an advantage over their rivals. It involved spying on adversaries' state secrets, scientific research, or major economic sectors, accumulating information that could benefit the perpetrating nation.

An instance that startled the world was the discovery of the "Stuxnet"' worm in 2010. This sophisticated malware was designed to sabotage Iran's nuclear program. It reportedly destroyed numerous centrifuges at Iran's Natanz nuclear facility, setting the program back by several years. Although no entity claimed responsibility, forensic investigations pointed towards a nation-state-level operation.

3.4. Organising for Cyber Defense

Recognizing the evolving threat landscape, nations started establishing dedicated cyber units. The United States formed Cyber

Command in 2009 to secure its digital frontier, while the United Kingdom launched the National Cyber Security Centre in 2016 for the same purpose. These entities used methods like intrusion detection, vulnerability assessment, and network security to protect state infrastructure.

Private sector organisations, too, began employing robust security measures like firewalls, encryption, and anomaly detection systems to fortify their digital fortresses. They recognised that the safety of their ecosystems was critical to maintain public trust and their commercial viability.

3.5. The Advent of Artificial Intelligence

In the last decade, another significant leap in cyber warfare has dwelled in artificial intelligence (AI). AI contributes to state-of-the-art defenses but also poses potential new threats. Predictive analytics and machine learning algorithms allow for the mitigation of cyber threats before they become widespread. At the same time, these modern tools in the wrong hands could anticipate and bypass even the most robust defensive digital ecosystems.

AI-enabled cyber attacks can execute swiftly and at massive scale. In addition, they can adapt to security protocols in real time, making them highly effective and hard to trace. On the defense side, AI can quickly sift through vast amounts of data, pinpointing anomalies and validating threats at unprecedented speeds.

3.6. The Future of Cyber Warfare

The future of cyber warfare resides at the intersection of technology, geopolitics, and national security. As more nation-states are acknowledging the cyber domain as a legitimate battlefield, we are witnessing a continuous arms race.

With the convergence of technologies like AI, Quantum Computing, and the Internet of Things (IoT), this arms race could mark a new phase in the evolution of cyber warfare. A world in which sophisticated technologies could be weaponized in ways we've yet to fully comprehend.

To conclude, the emergence and subsequent evolution of cyber warfare manifest both the innovative prowess and destructive potential of human endeavour in the digital era. Cyber warfare has come a long way from its rudimentary beginnings, and its future forecasts little sign of slowing down. In this new battleground, strategy matters as much as strength, vigilance is a virtue, and the front lines are just one click away.

Chapter 4. Interaction of AI and Cyber Warfare: An Overview

Artificial Intelligence (AI) and Cyber Warfare are two domains that continue to gain momentum in the arena of technological innovation and strategic defense. The increasing complexity of cyber threats paired with the rapid advancements in AI technology have organically gravitated toward each other, leading to the amalgamation of two prolific domains. Below are the details of how this interplay unfolds and influences the realm of global security and defense.

4.1. AI: Redefining Defense Mechanisms

There is a substantial shift in defense strategies corresponding to the advent of AI. The implications of AI in cyber defense are far-reaching, affecting numerous components of a standard security set-up. The ability of AI to process large volumes of data and learn patterns enhances prevention, detection, and resolution of cyber threats.

Automation and Machine Learning (ML), subsets of AI, can improve efficiency by performing tedious tasks and analyzing vast datasets, respectively. As adversaries grow increasingly sophisticated, AI can keep pace and adapt to new threats. AI has also enabled a paradigm shift from reactive security measures to proactive ones, predicting threats before they manifest fully.

4.2. Cyber Warfare: Breach of Digital Borders

Cyber Warfare is the virtual battleground where offensive and defensive strategies are implemented to protect or compromise digital assets. It has distinct characteristics that set it apart from traditional warfare. Cyber attacks, unlike physical attacks, occur at lightning speed and can originate from anywhere, given the boundary-less nature of the digital realm.

Cyber Warfare is made increasingly complex due to the diversification of threats - from Distributed Denial of Service (DDoS) attacks to Advanced Persistent Threats (APT). Nation-states, cybercriminals, and hacktivists employ an array of techniques, including malware, ransomware, and phishing, leading to substantial economic, political, and social impact.

4.3. Cyber Intelligence: Information Gathering and Threat Detection

Underpinning successful cyber defense is Cyber Intelligence - the information that helps identify potential threats, active attacks, and their sources. Intelligence gathering has been substantially bolstered by AI algorithms, which can parse vast amounts of data from diverse sources in record time.

AI is changing the very face of Cyber Intelligence. With ML, an AI system can learn from previous threats and predict future ones, even those hidden in large streams of operational data. This is notably beneficial in preventing zero-day exploits, where vulnerabilities unknown to software vendors are exploited by adversaries before they can be patched.

4.4. AI in Offensive Cyber Warfare

AI's contributions to cyber warfare are not limited to defense. It can also be used offensively, becoming a tool in the hands of hackers or nation-states aiming to use cyber warfare for their advantage. The potential for AI to automate attacks or enhance their effectiveness is a major concern for global security.

Botnet attacks, for instance, could escalate in potency through the use of AI. Machine learning algorithms could correlate data from various sources to identify weak spots in a system and coordinate attacks, achieving much higher efficiency than human hackers alone.

4.5. The Double-Edged Sword: Ethics and AI in Cyber Warfare

Bringing together AI and Cyber Warfare inevitably evokes a critical debate centered around ethics. The use of lethal autonomous weapons (LAWs) in warfare is a contentious issue, raising dilemmas surrounding accountability, legality, and transparency. For instance, should an AI-controlled system fail, determining accountability becomes complex, with potential blame allocated to the AI designers, operators, or system itself.

In Cyber Warfare, similar dilemmas arise with offensive AI. AI-driven attacks can attribute anonymity to the attacker, which raises legal implications. Also, the potential for collateral damage is significant if AI systems are not properly controlled.

4.6. Final Thoughts: The Dynamic Intersection of AI and Cyber Warfare

The intersection of AI and Cyber Warfare is indeed, a complex crossroad that balances immense potential benefits against escalating threats. AI, with its ability to learn and adapt, can revolutionize cyber defense and intelligence, providing a much-needed boost in a rapidly evolving threat landscape. On the other hand, the propensity for AI to be misused in cyber attacks underscores the urgency to establish legal and ethical guidelines.

This multifaceted interplay showcases a captivating, albeit challenging, chapter of the book of modern defense. As AI continues to evolve, so too will its role in Cyber Warfare, requiring continuous vigilance, regulation, and understanding. The intricacies of this interplay will likely dictate significant aspects of global security, defense, and warfare in the near future.

Chapter 5. The Mechanisms of AI in Cyber Defense

Artificial intelligence (AI) has become a cornerstone in cyber defense strategies, providing a proactive and automated means to defend against cyber threats. Fueled by the rapid growth and sophistication of cyber threats, and the increasing digitization of societies, the need for AI defenses in cyber warfare is more crucial than ever. The successful integration of AI into cyber defense mechanisms hinges on the understanding and implementation of several important concepts.

5.1. AI Capabilities and Cyber Threats

At its core, AI is a machine's ability to mimic human intelligence processes, including learning from experiences, reasoning, understanding language, recognizing patterns, and problem-solving. In the context of cyber defense, these capabilities allow AI to anticipate, identify, and counteract cyber threats with greater speed and efficiency than traditional cybersecurity measures.

AI-powered security systems can analyze vast amounts of data in real-time, detecting anomalies that might indicate a cyber threat. They can also predict future threats based on historical data and trend analysis. So, AI effectively transforms cyber defense from a reactive process (i.e., responding to an attack after it occurs) to a proactive one (i.e., preventing attacks from even occurring).

5.2. Machine Learning in Cyber Defense

Machine Learning (ML), a subset of AI, plays a pivotal role in modern cyber defense strategies. ML algorithms can learn from and make decisions based on data, enabling systems to adapt to new threats faster. Unlike traditional rule-based security systems, ML-powered defenses can evolve autonomously, adjusting their defenses to combat new threats as they emerge.

Two types of machine learning particularly useful in cyber defense are supervised learning and unsupervised learning. Supervised learning requires labeled datasets and is adept at classification and regression tasks. For instance, it can classify network traffic as 'normal' or 'malicious' based on historical data. Unsupervised learning, on the other hand, doesn't require labeled data. It identifies anomalies or outliers in a dataset, making it particularly adept at detecting unknown threats or zero-day exploits through anomaly detection.

5.3. Natural Language Processing in Cyber Defense

Natural Language Processing (NLP), another subset of AI, is used to understand and decipher human language in text or spoken form. In the domain of cyber defense, NLP can be used for threat intelligence gathering and cybersecurity analytics.

One of its applications is in parsing and interpreting unstructured data from various sources such as online forums, blog posts, news articles, and social media posts. NLP can process this information, extracting relevant cyber threat indicators (IP addresses, URLs, email addresses, malware names, etc.) and threat actor TTPs (Tactics, Techniques, and Procedures). This intelligence can then inform

15

defensive measures against potential cyber threats.

Apart from threat intelligence, NLP can assist in automating and speeding up incident response. When a security breach occurs, incident reports are often created in natural language. NLP can interpret these reports, extracting vital details and prioritizing responses based on severity.

5.4. Deep Learning in Cyber Defense

Deep Learning (DL), another subset of AI, is inspired by the functioning of the human brain. It uses layered neural networks to solve complex patterns in datasets too large and complicated for human understanding. In cyber defense, deep learning helps in detecting potentially harmful activities by recognizing patterns in vast volumes of data.

Convolutional Neural Networks (CNNs), a type of deep learning model, are particularly effective at image and video processing. They can be utilized to detect phishing websites by analyzing the site's images and identifying discrepancies that might suggest a fraudulent page.

Recurrent Neural Networks (RNNs), another type of deep learning model, analyze sequential data, making them excellent for time-series data analysis like network traffic or user behavior.

5.5. Limitations and Challenges in AI for Cyber Defense

Despite the capabilities of AI in cyber defense, there are inherent limitations and challenges in its deployment. For instance, while ML models are proficient at recognizing threats they were trained on, they may struggle to identify novel, unseen threats.

Additionally, AI and ML models are vulnerable to adversarial attacks, where malicious actors manipulate the input data to trick the model into making incorrect predictions. Cyber defenders need to secure their AI and machine learning models to ensure their accuracy and robustness.

AI-powered cyber defense requires immense computational power and vast datasets for training. However, the acquisition, processing, and storage of such data can raise privacy and ethical concerns, especially when personal and sensitive data is involved.

Yet, the benefits of AI in cyber defense significantly outweigh the challenges. The creative use of AI not only enhances our capacity to predict and respond to cyber threats but also could redefine the dynamics of cybersecurity by shifting the advantage from the attackers to the defenders.

5.6. Conclusion

The integration of AI into cyber defense mechanisms is a complex process that requires understanding and careful implementation. When appropriately leveraged, these technologies can provide a comprehensive, efficient, and responsive defense system capable of identifying and combatting rising cyber threats. As AI technologies continue to improve, the capabilities they offer in cyber defense are expected to become increasingly sophisticated, helping us keep pace with the evolving landscape of cyber warfare.

Chapter 6. New Terrain: The Impact of AI on Cyber Tactics

Understanding the landscape in which cyber warfare operates is the first step to realizing the profound effect AI holds on this arena. Hence, to gain a rigorous grasp of such a terrain, it's essential to build a solid foundation by exploring the traditional methods previously employed in cyber warfare.

Borders once so clearly defined in the flesh-and-blood warfare have fumbled into obsolescence in cyber warfare, and the physically distanced can interact in a blink. Before delving into AI's impact, it's noteworthy to understand these alterations and their implications.

6.1. Traditional Cyber Warfare Tactics

In essence, traditional cyber warfare exercises encompass tactics such as espionage, sabotage, propaganda dissemination, data breach, and even physical damage to infrastructure. For instance, a major national electricity grid could be targeted by rival allegiances, intending to bring about chaos. Intelligence agencies could infiltrate government networks to steal classified information, a process known as cyber espionage.

These tactics, however disruptive, have a significant drawback: the human element. Highly trained personnel are required, capable of delicate and precise operations. While these specialists are not short in supply, they naturally operate at a human pace, requiring days or even months to strategize, plan, and execute these digital combat missions meticulously.

Enter Artificial Intelligence, a game-changer, capable of not only executing given assignments but also learning on its way.

6.2. AI: Bringing Efficiency and Scale

While the cyber warfare landscape was evolving, the technological advancements breathed life into the concept of Artificial Intelligence. The basic premise of AI—in essence, machines learning to think and act like humans—thrust the lever from human-limited operations to efficient, scalable solutions which did not tire, falter, or require meal breaks.

AI systems can parse large amounts of data quickly, identify patterns, make predictions, and adapt behaviour based on these findings — all at a superhuman pace and scale. This bears immediate relevance in cyber warfare, where vast digital terrains must be combed for vulnerabilities, patterns, or signs of enemy activity.

Furthermore, the AI's learning agility enables a much faster response time to triggers, effectively reducing the impact of an attack. If a specific pattern of activities was identified and linked to an attack, the AI would take instant measures during its recurrence. This 'response metric' is transforming how we perceive and counter cyber threats.

6.3. AI in Offensive Operations

AI's impact on cyber attacks is twofold: it has become an ally and enemy. On the offensive front, AI tools can automate and execute complex attacks with larger usage footprints than human hackers could achieve. The infamous example of such is DeepLocker, a model designed by IBM that used AI to conduct targeted attacks, avoiding detection until the specific target had been reached.

Virtual armies of 'bots' can be created to amplify the attack's strength, overwhelming and potentially crippling the targeted situations before any meaningful defense can be mounted. Moreover, these bots can also be instructed to behave like normal digital traffic, eluding traditional firewalls and intrusion detection systems.

6.4. AI in Defensive Operations

While AI's offensive use is daunting, it's also proving a formidable defense tool. Security professionals use AI and machine learning algorithms to monitor and analyze network activity, promptly identifying unusual patterns that could indicate a breach. An AI system can learn what 'normal' activity appears like on a specific network and immediately red-flag deviations.

Incident response times have been drastically reduced thanks to these alert systems. Plus, AI can often isolate the intruder and prevent them from causing further damage. AI has also paved a way for proactive defense, predicting attacks before they occur based on learned patterns.

In essence, AI's capabilities for rapid intrusion detection and response, coupled with the creation of robust automated defense systems, herald a new era in cybersecurity. The battlefield has evolved at a dramatic pace, with AI bringing a paradigm shift. Understanding its implications becomes a prerequisite in securing our future in the digital universe.

6.5. Conclusion: The AI-transformed Terrain

Cyber warfare has witnessed a transformation over the decades, effectively reshaping how technology and defense tactics intertwine. With AI stepping up the game, the cyber warfare terrain has morphed into a new one, where attacks and defenses aren't merely conducted—they're intelligently designed, automated, and endlessly learning.

While the multiplicity of AI's applications unravels new opportunities, it also uncovers fresh threats. As we venture further into the age of AI, we see once clearly defined lines blurred. Artificial Intelligence, despite its tool-like nature, has in essence become a combatant in itself.

This AI-transformed landscape beholds both perils and opportunities: the scale and efficiency of AI operations have raised concerns over potential misuse, but evidence of its effective utilization for our defense serves as a beacon of promise.

Understanding the ever-evolving field of AI in cyber warfare becomes a survival necessity, and it is our collective responsibility to ensure this lifeline's evolution doesn't come at our peril but translates into opportunities for a safer world. AI has opened a Pandora's box, yes, bittersweet, yet brimming with untapped potentials. As we close the narrative on its current impact, our eye is inherently drawn to what's next. In the forthcoming sections, the exploration continues—farther and deeper into the implications and possibilities in the realm of artificial intelligence. Stay tuned, as your journey into the labyrinth of cyber warfare is only getting started.

Chapter 7. The Real-time Battle: AI's Transformative Role in Threat Detection

In the annals of warfare, there has always been a race to employ the latest technological advancements on the battlefield. Today, the battlefield has transcended its physical domain into a realm of bytes and bits, where nations clash in a new form of warfare - cyber warfare. Here can be found an epic and stealthy struggle, a real-time battle being played out across our interconnected infrastructure. These modern battlefields have emerged as significant, complex data environments, where artificial intelligence (AI) is increasingly playing a defining role in threat detection and response.

7.1. Emerging Threat Landscape

Before AI's entry, cyber security was primarily the terrain of signature-based and rule-based threat detection systems. However, these systems' Achilles heel lies in their inability to cope with novel threats and their dependence on predefined rules. In this new landscape of sophistications, cyber threats are intricate, mutating and multi-faceted. Zero-day vulnerabilities come to light abruptly, and attacks are no longer isolated incidents that levy brute force, but skillful, crafty intrusions that skillfully maneuver through a system's defenses.

7.2. Real-time Defence: When every Second Counts

In the face of these growing complexities and high stakes, AI emerges as the arsenal that nations need, an ever-watchful guardian that never sleeps. AI, with its machine learning capabilities, evolves, learns, and adapts to changing threat scenarios, offering a real-time defense to perpetual threats. Armed with rapid processing speeds, it helps detect threats faster than any human, achieving an efficiency and speed that effectively staves off cyber attacks. When every second counts, AI becomes undeniably crucial for nations' cyber strategies and defenses.

7.3. AI's Application in Threat Detection

Machine Learning (ML), a subset of AI, plays a pivotal role in threat detection. Through the use of ML algorithms, AI models can learn from historical cyber attack data and pattern recognition to predict and identify possible future attacks. The AI models' predictive capabilities improve as their exposure to data increases, these models gaining the ability to detect even elusive and subtle patterns that human analysts might overlook. Such systems also constantly scan an organization's networked systems, enabling proactive defense and allowing organizations to strategize and instantiate response plans before attackers have a foothold.

7.4. Adapting to Unknown Threats: The Power of Unsupervised Learning

One key advantage that AI has over traditional threat detection systems is its adaptability to unknown threats. Unsupervised Machine Learning algorithms learn from data without prior training, unlike their supervised counterparts. These algorithms are capable of identifying outliers or anomalies in large data sets, thus effectively picking out suspicious activities from everyday operations in a network. This helps in recognizing and managing new types of cyber threats, adapting to evolving cyber attack strategies and thereby ensuring an organization's preparedness in an ever-changing cyberspace landscape.

7.5. Autonomous Response: Taking Action

AI does not limit itself to detecting potential threats; it goes a step further and plays a proactive role in responding to them. Thanks to AI's capabilities, we are seeing the rise of autonomous defenses, systems capable of responding to threats in real time. For instance, AI can instantly isolate a compromised node on a network, limiting the potential damage caused by a breach. In a more extreme scenario, the capabilities of AI extend to designing and launching pre-emptive strikes on sources of potential threats, thus inherently discouraging cyber attackers.

7.6. Human-AI Partnership: The Resilient Shield

However, despite the myriad advantages AI brings, a totally AI-dependent approach is not the most effective strategy. While AI greatly augments the cyber defense workflow, human knowledge and intuition continue to play a vital role in understanding and managing complex threat landscapes. A partnership of human experience with AI's processing power and capabilities offers the best blend of speed, efficiency, and nuanced understanding.

The real-time battle of cyber warfare is being effectively fought with AI now leading the charge. By harnessing its power to detect, predict, and respond to looming threats, we are actively reshaping our cyber defense strategies. Yet, it's fundamental to remember that while AI is a powerful tool in this combat, it should be treated as a complement to, rather than a replacement for, human ingenuity and experience. In such a partnership, resilience to cyber threats becomes a tangible reality.

As the AI-centered approach to cyber defense continues to evolve, its strengths and weaknesses will become even more evident. But for now, the consensus is clear: AI is a formidable ally in this real-time battle against cyber threats, a guardian in the byte and bit filled trenches of cyber warfare. An ally we will increasingly depend on as the shape of warfare continues to metamorphose in this digital age.

Chapter 8. Escalation: How AI Elevates Cyber Offense and Defense

Artificial intelligence (AI) has emerged as a formidable force in the realm of cyber offense and defense. Its swift rise to prominence offers both profound opportunities and unprecedented challenges. An understanding of this dual-natured technology is crucial as we anticipate the next steps in this continually evolving domain. To help in this endeavor, we will explore how AI has raised the bar for both cyber offense and defense.

8.1. The Rise of AI in Cyber Offensive Tactics

As AI permeates cyber strategies, we're seeing an upswing in offensive applications. Perfidious actors are aware of AI's potential to wreak havoc and are leveraging this technology to enhance the sophistication, scale, and effectiveness of their attacks.

An early sign of this escalation is the appearance of AI-powered malware. These malicious pieces of code now transcend simple payload delivery and employ AI to create adaptive, self-evolving threats that can bypass antivirus solutions. Notably, AI assists malware in blending with routine network traffic, making detection incredibly difficult.

AI can automate the execution of 'spear-phishing' techniques, for example, that are usually time-consuming and resource-intensive. Such methods yield high success rates by feeding on recipients' psychological vulnerabilities. With the added layer of AI, these attacks can now be personalized and scaled up, significantly expanding the potential attack surface, thus transforming an already potent threat into an industrial-scale operation.

The use of AI isn't restricted to improved execution. A case in point is Deepfake technology, manipulatively used to fabricate or morph digital content. AI-powered Deepfakes, whether audio, video, or text, represent a technological leap in the creation of false information and could become invaluable tools for strategic disinformation campaigns. The operation of such campaigns can disrupt societies on a vast scale, destabilizing politics, and introducing chaos within the military or financial systems.

8.2. AI-Driven Escalation in Cyber Defense

On the flip side, AI is proving instrumental in mounting advanced cyber defensive mechanisms to counteract evolving threats. Cyber defense platforms powered by AI are being developed to anticipate, detect, and neutralize malicious activities, thereby reshaping the cyber security landscape.

One of the most significant contributions of AI lies in anomaly detection. AI algorithms, with machine learning at their core, can be trained to study network traffic patterns and develop a normative model. Once the model is established, any deviation is easily detected, alerting the system to a potential breach.

AI also accelerates incident response times. Widespread networks generate copious amounts of data, which, when overseen by human analysts alone, can lead to extensive response wait times. AI can rummage through this data at high speed, combing for anomalies and accelerating the risk mitigation process.

Furthermore, AI is increasingly being utilized for threat intelligence, predictive analytics, and threat hunting. By processing vast data sets,

AI can identify trends, predict cyber threats in advance, and even track the source of an attack. When integrated with a proactive threat-hunting approach, this can turn the tables on adversaries, allowing defenders to isolate their operations and even mount counter-offensives.

AI's role in cyber defense goes beyond technical arenas into strategizing and decision-making. AI-powered security orchestration, automation, and response (SOAR) systems enable security teams to prioritize and standardize responses to cyber threats. It helps in coordinating human and machine efforts, thereby achieving peak proficiency in defense tactics.

8.3. Dual-Edged Sword: The AI Paradox

As we traverse this novel landscape, the dichotomy of AI becomes evident. We're witnessing a twofold escalation—an arms race—where advances in AI-powered threat measures instigate progress in counteracting defenses. It's truly a manifestation of Yin and Yang, emulating an ever-lasting cycle of action and reaction.

The future of cyber warfare, therefore, rests on the understanding and harnessing of AI and its capabilities. Such an appreciation is key to maintaining balance, averting the potential for AI to be weaponized unrestrainedly, and securing the infinite array of networks that form the scaffold of modern society.

As technology advances unrelentingly, the onus is on us to remain cognizant of these shifts, to adapt, and to evolve. Such is the quintessence of survival in the cybernetic era. Tread carefully, for the landscape is complex. Yet, by committing to continuous learning and anticipating the curveballs of the future, one can indeed navigate this challenging terrain.

Chapter 9. Ethical Dilemmas and Legal Aspects of AI in Cyber Warfare

Our exploration of AI in cyber warfare now leads us to an intriguing intersection where ethics and legality meet technology. Framing this discourse requires understanding that while AI can amplify our cybersecurity measures, its misuse can potentially escalate conflicts and create geopolitical tensions. This chapter sheds light on the myriad ethical dilemmas and legal complexities surrounding AI in cyber warfare and discusses potential ramifications.

9.1. The Ethical Conundrum

AI technology is disrupting norms and regulations across multiple sectors, and cyber warfare is no exception. The ethical challenges posed by the integration of AI into this realm are complex, contingent on the specifics of its utilization, the intent behind its application, and the downstream effects of its deployment.

One significant ethical challenge revolves around the autonomy given to AI systems. As experts continue to develop sophisticated AI tools for cyber warfare, the decision-making process in the deployment of such tools is increasingly delegated to algorithms. The latitude given to AI, in such scenarios, is unprecedented, and it raises ethical concerns about accountability. It begs the question: who is accountable when AI-driven cyber warfare results in unintended consequences? This accountability extends beyond immediate harm to encompass potential escalations of virtual hostilities into real-world conflicts.

Beyond accountability, the inherent nature of AI—its processing of large amounts of data, its propensity to learn from new information, and its capability to act beyond its initial programming—raises significant concerns about privacy and data security. In an age where personal data is continuously mined, stored, and monetized, the increased integration of AI into cyber defense can potentially exacerbate privacy breaches. The ethical implications of sacrificing privacy for security need to be carefully assessed in this light.

9.2. The Legal Quagmire

Aside from the ethical complexities, the legislation related to AI in cyber warfare is also murky at best, due to various reasons. Firstly, the rapid development and deployment of AI technologies have essentially outpaced existing legal structures. Laws and regulations that were designed to deal with conventional warfare and traditional cybersecurity threats often find themselves overwhelmed by the unique challenges presented by AI.

Secondly, the intrinsic global nature of cyber warfare makes it even more difficult for national or even international legal frameworks to effectively manage or govern. The transnational nature of cyber attacks, enabled by AI, means that they aren't particularly restricted by geopolitical boundaries. This poses a monumental challenge to legislation.

Moreover, the asymmetry in AI capabilities among nations causes an uneven playing field in cyber warfare. This is accompanied by an inherent difficulty in attributing cyberattacks accurately, leading to ambiguity and reduced enforcement of laws and norms. Also, the concept of what constitutes a proportional response to cyber attacks is not uniformly defined, further confounding the legal discourse.

9.3. A Path Forward: Policy Recommendations

To negotiate these ethical dilemmas and legal complexities, it's critical to formulate sound policies that balance technological advancements with ethical norms and legal safeguards. Here are a few recommendations:

1. Emphasize Transparency and Accountability: AI systems should be designed to allow scrutiny and review of their decisions where possible. The inner workings of AI systems need to be transparent, as this is crucial for assigning liability and ensuring accountability.

2. Promote International Cooperation: The transnational nature of cyber warfare suggests that international collaboration is crucial. Encouraging normative behavior in cyberspace, sharing strategies for mitigating threats, and facilitating dialogue on AI's implication in cyber warfare should be high on the international agenda.

3. Establish Legal Frameworks: Such frameworks should reflect the realities of AI applications in cyber warfare and provide clear guidance on AI utilization. It's advisable for all nations to understand and anticipate the impacts of AI-driven cyber warfare and structure laws accordingly.

Navigating the uncharted waters of AI in cyber warfare is a daunting task. But with careful attention to ethical considerations and legal aspects, we can ensure a relatively safe transition into this new era of defense technology. The power of AI comes with great responsibilities and challenges, making this discourse not just relevant for today, but crucial for the decades to come.

Chapter 10. Case Studies: AI in Modern Cybersecurity Operations

Artificial intelligence is no longer confined to the realms of academia and industry; it's now an essential tool for modern cyber warfare. What follows are case studies that illustrate the definitive role of AI in strategic cybersecurity operations across the globe.

10.1. The Defense Advanced Research Projects Agency (DARPA) and Automated Cyber Defense

One of the earliest instances of AI application in cybersecurity is the Cyber Grand Challenge organized by DARPA in 2016. DARPA, a pioneer in AI and ML technologies since the 1960s, conducted the first-ever machine-only Capture the Flag contest. In this challenge, seven automated systems competed to identify vulnerabilities, create patches, and employ strategies against the opponents in real-time.

The winner of the competition was 'Mayhem', a supercomputer developed by ForAllSecure. 'Mayhem' exhibited an exceptional ability to detect, evaluate, and patch vulnerabilities in a complex and evolving network environment, outperforming all its competitors. This event showcased the growth of AI in automatic vulnerability detection and patching, a crucial component in any robust cybersecurity approach.

10.2. The IBM Watson and Cognitive Security

In 2011, IBM stunned the world when their AI system, Watson, succeeded in defeating human champions in the game show, Jeopardy. Watson's advanced natural language processing, data integration, and machine learning capabilities now serve a critical role in cybersecurity.

In 2016, IBM revealed that Watson had been trained in cyber security language using over one million security documents. The Watson for Cyber Security project is considered one of the leading advancements in cognitive AI-based security. Watson's huge analytical power aids in filtering out false positives and categorizing threats, thereby reducing response times and enabling real-time threat intelligence.

10.3. Darktrace and The Enterprise Immune System

UK-based cyber defense company Darktrace employs AI in an innovative way. Their product, the Enterprise Immune System technology, utilizes machine learning algorithms to autonomously identify and respond to cyber threats.

By deploying this technology on networks, Darktrace claims to mimic the human immune system's behavior, learning what is normal for a particular system and identifying anomalies. This proactive approach to cyber defense has successfully identified and stopped threats like insider attacks and zero-day exploits.

10.4. CrowdStrike and AI-Powered Threat Detection

American cybersecurity technology company CrowdStrike is pushing AI frontiers in threat detection. Their Falcon platform uses AI to deliver real-time protection and instantaneous threat detection. Through leveraging the speed of cloud-scale AI, CrowdStrike investigates billions of events in real-time daily, enabling companies to respond to threats within the blink of an eye.

10.5. Gmail and AI-Based Phishing Protections

Even everyday applications like Google's Gmail use AI to enhance their security operations. Utilizing machine learning algorithms to recognize the patterns in phishing attacks, Gmail effectively filters insidious emails, preventing them from reaching the user inbox. This AI-based defense actively learns from new attacks, improving the system's protection capabilities over time.

The aforementioned case studies represent just the tip of the iceberg when it comes to AI in modern cyber defense operations. What comes across clearly is the growing reliance on AI in detecting and countering cyber threats, given its inherent capability to analyze and learn from large, complex data sets at a pace beyond human capacity. However, it is vital to recognize the limitations and potential vulnerabilities: an AI is only as good as the data it learns from, and all systems, AI-included, carry intrinsic risks which need to be accounted for in the incessant fight against cyber threats.

As we journey further into this digital age, it's crucial to keep pace with rapid technological advancements. The AI-enriched cybersecurity landscape presents a revolutionary, yet challenging domain to navigate. Nonetheless, as long as we continue to invest in intelligent cybersecurity tactics, we will undoubtedly progress towards a more secure future.

Chapter 11. Looking Ahead: Future Developments in AI and Cyber Warfare

Today, every socio-political discourse, every strategic development in national security, finds its roots interlinked with the technological advancements we bear witness to. The spotlight that was once pointed at nuclear capabilities has shifted its focus towards the unbound expanse of cyber warfare. With the ingress of artificial intelligence (AI) in this domain, the paths being beaten have raised more questions than they have answered, being unpredictable in their impact and profound in their implications.

11.1. The Accelerated Evolution of AI

Presently, we find ourselves at a crossroad where AI has already begun to extend beyond rudimentary systems to implementations capable of complex decision-making processes and cognition-like abilities. The past decade itself has seen the burgeoning of technologies like deep learning and reinforcement learning. Simply put, AI systems are increasingly imbibing human-like attributes including, but not limited to, sensory understanding, autonomous decision-making, and faster-than-human reaction times.

In the realm of cybersecurity, these capabilities are being employed for myriad applications, from detecting anomalous behavior in network traffic to formulating dynamic defense strategies and taking real-time action against security threats. Increasingly sophisticated AI models are capable of predicting, identifying, and neutralizing threats before they're even fully realized. With each passing day, AI systems are getting ingrained more deeply into cyber defense mechanisms.

11.2. The Cyberspace Battlefield: Where AI Meets Cyber Warfare

As we meander down the timeline, the concept of warfare has morphically evolved, with the advent of virtual cyberspace acting as a new battleground. We witness an era where conflicts are not confined to geographical boundaries. The tapestry of warfare has been subtly woven into the fabric of the digital world, and its importance cannot be underplayed.

The application of AI to cyber warfare has given rise to the concept of autonomous cyber weapons. In essence, these are AI systems capable of identifying targets independently, devising attack strategies, and executing them without human intervention. The pace at which this new warfare paradigm evolves vastly outstrips that of conventional battle landscape. This accelerated evolution, paired with the limitless expanse of the cyberspace, creates a new-age threat landscape that is incredibly volatile.

11.3. AI-Enabled Defense Techniques in Cyber Warfare

As technology advances, so too does the sophistication of cyberattacks. However, the same evolution also empowers the defenses. AI and machine learning (ML) have been integrated with cyber defense systems, where they can learn from each interaction, acquiring valuable skills to counter even the most dynamic cyber threats.

The techniques employed are variegated, encompassing intrusion detection systems (IDS) that use ML to identify striking patterns or anomalies within the network traffic, predictive modeling that preemptively charts the characteristics of potential threats, AI-powered firewalls that provide an added layer of security, and Automated threat hunting, where AI is leveraged to detect hidden threats by analyzing patterns and anomalies.

Additionally, AI allows the creation and simulation of 'honeypots': traps designed to detect, deflect or study attempts at unauthorized utilization of information systems, often taking the form of seemingly vulnerable systems intended to act as lures for attackers.

11.4. Potential Pitfalls and Ethical Considerations

With the ascendancy of AI-based solutions in cyber warfare, there's an increasing emphasis on understanding the potential pitfalls and ethical considerations that arise. Autonomous cyber warfare systems risk negating human accountability, leading to a potential 'responsibility gap' when things go wrong.

Moreover, the dual-use nature of AI technology, usable for both defensive and offensive purposes, raises concerns about misuse. The democratization and widespread accessibility of potent AI tools pose the risk of falling into the wrong hands.

From an ethical perspective, this raises concerns about the 'line in the sand' where autonomous AI systems are concerned. AI slated for cyber warfare requires rigorous vetting and consistent regulation, though defining the limits and implementing them remains increasingly complex.

11.5. The Horizon: AI and Cyber Warfare

Looking ahead, AI stands like an unharnessed entity on the expanse of cyber warfare. We may soon witness AI systems capable of learning and creating new strategies dynamically in real-time, presenting a multifold increase in the complexity of attack and defense situations.

However, it is crucial to remember that the raw computational power of AI doesn't replace the creativity, intuition, and understanding of context that inherent human intelligence brings to the table. Cybersecurity is not just about speed and accuracy but also about understanding the 'meta' rules of the game, something that autonomous AI systems might fall short of.

In summary, the future development of AI and its integration in cyber warfare is imperative but needs to be carefully balanced with strategic human oversight. Not only does it require the continual evolution of technology but also a comprehensive socio-ethical framework to ensure its secure deployment. The compass guiding future developments will be set not merely on the basis of scientific advancements but equally, if not more, by the ethical and legal constructs of societies worldwide. This balance will form the linchpin as we venture deeper into the world of AI and cyber warfare.

www.ingramcontent.com/pod-product-compliance
Lightning Source LLC
Chambersburg PA
CBHW061055050326

40690CB00012B/2637